Daily Writing Fundamentals

Grades 11–12

 **WALCH PUBLISHING**

Strategic Teaching Books, Inc.

SGS-SFI/COC-US09/5501

1   2   3   4   5   6   7   8   9   10

ISBN 978-0-8251-6269-5

Copyright © 2007

J. Weston Walch, Publisher

www.walch.com

P.O. Box 658 • Portland, Maine 04104-0658

Printed in the United States of America

Introduction

What is *Daily Writing Fundamentals*?

Daily Writing Fundamentals is a series designed to enhance your current writing curriculum. Comprised of four books for grades 5–6, 7–8, 9–10, and 11–12, each volume includes student grade-level writing examples, as well as selections from well-known authors. The student examples have been gathered from over 30 years of teaching, and have been edited and revised throughout the years.

Developed by a group of five experienced language arts teachers, trainers, and literacy specialists, these brief daily writing activities can fit into any classroom schedule.

Daily Writing Fundamentals is best practice!

Writing is a task that can be challenging for students to master. Other than grammar and mechanics, it is a skill closely connected to reading and critical thinking. Writing difficulties can be overcome through a variety of engaging activities such as making writing a collaborative experience. Most students enjoy reading and discussing other students' writing; it provides them with a sense of security, and may allow a greater sense of ease when analyzing and sharing their own writing.

Try the following best practices in your classroom:

- Study, evaluate, and discuss models of good writing with students.
- Provide students with opportunities to reflect on what good writing is and how writing can be improved.
- Encourage students to spend sufficient time on a piece of writing to learn from it.
- Have students write often and in every class.

Daily Writing Fundamentals is designed around these practices to provide helpful models that will encourage your students to think about writing, to improve their own writing, and to make the art of writing part of their own lifelong learning goals.

(continued)

Using *Daily Writing Fundamentals*

The 32 weekly units are very flexible. Units can be adapted, questions can be combined, and you should feel free to add questions of your own. You may want to write the daily question on the board or on an overhead, or you can copy the five weekly questions and distribute them to students. Ample space has been provided throughout the book for you and your students to make notes.

The majority of the activities will only take your students a few minutes to complete. Some selections may take longer. Consider assigning these as homework.

The selections are numbered but don't have to be used in sequence. To focus on particular skill areas, use the convenient skill chart to find which selections address your students' needs.

Note: It is important to review each selection before use with your class. Because the student examples have been gathered from real-life experiences, some students may be sensitive to the content.

Skill Chart

Skill	Selection	Skill	Selection	Skill	Selection
Analyzing writing	1, 2, 6, 18, 30	Generating effective ideas	7, 10, 13, 21, 25	Sentence combining	14
Argumentation	18	Genre	6	Sentence structure/fluency	31, 32
Audience awareness	1, 28, 29	Organization	3, 6, 7, 13, 18, 29, 31	Setting	10, 26
Author's purpose	1	Paragraph development	5, 26	Sharing	16, 26
Business letter	29	Paraphrasing	17	Spelling	14
Capitalization	12, 19	Persuasive form	32	Subject/verb agreement	9
Categorizing	7	Poetry	2, 5, 22	Supporting details	6, 9, 18, 23, 28, 31
Characterization	26	Point of view	1	Tense	3, 10, 11, 30
Compare/contrast	2	Pronoun/antecedent agreement	9, 18	Theme/ideas	3, 9, 18, 23
Dialogue	26	Prose	30	Thesis	3
Effective development	1	Punctuation	6, 8, 12, 14, 19	Tone/voice	10, 14, 32
Effective introduction	23, 31	Reflection	27	Transitions	9
Effective conclusion	9, 14, 18, 23, 28	Repetition	30	Usage	15, 24
Experimenting with form	22	Responding to a prompt	3, 14, 16	Using writing models	22
Experimenting with language	5, 26	Résumé/college application	4	Word choice	1, 28, 32
Figurative language	1, 30	Revision	5, 7, 10, 16, 17, 18, 22, 23, 26, 28, 29	Writing response groups	20, 26, 32

Selection 1

[1] The bee is in the main an honest citizen; she prefers legitimate to illegitimate business; she is never an outlaw until her proper sources of supply fail; she will not touch honey as long as honey-yielding flowers can be found; she always prefers to go to the fountain-head, and dislikes to take her sweets at second hand. [2] But in the fall, after the flowers have failed, she can be tempted. [3] The bee-hunter takes advantage of this fact; he betrays her with a little honey. [4] He wants to steal her stores, and he first encourages her to steal his, then follows the thief home with her booty. [5] This is the whole trick of the bee-hunter. [6] The bees never suspect his game, else by taking a circuitous route they could easily baffle him. [7] But the honey-bee has absolutely no wit or cunning outside of her special gifts as a gatherer and storer of honey. [8] She is a simple-minded creature, and can be imposed upon by any novice. [9] Yet it is not every novice that can find a bee-tree. [10] The sportsman may track his game to its retreat by the aid of his dog, but in hunting the honey-bee one must be his own dog, and track his game through an element in which it leaves no trail. [11] It is a task for a sharp, quick eye, and may test the resources of the best wood-craft. [12] One autumn when I devoted much time to this pursuit, as the best means of getting at nature and the open-air exhilaration, my eye became so trained that bees were nearly as easy to it as birds. [13] I saw and heard bees wherever I went. [14] One day, standing on a street corner in a great city, I saw above the trucks and the traffic a line of bees carrying off sweets from some grocery or confectionery shop.

—*Birds and Bees, Sharp Eyes and Other Papers,*
John Burroughs, 1837–1921

Selection 1

Daily Student Prompts

DAY 1

How does the writer personify the bee in this paragraph? What does this accomplish, and how does it affect the reader?

DAY 2

From what viewpoint is this paragraph written (first person, second person, and third person—singular or plural)? Why was it necessary for the author to use this viewpoint?

DAY 3

Select five nouns that are especially effective. What less-specific nouns could the author have used in place of the five nouns? How do the replacement nouns weaken the paragraph?

DAY 4

What was the author's purpose in writing this piece? What current publication would print this type of selection?

DAY 5

Do you believe the author's statement in line 14? Defend your answer. Why would the author have included this sentence?

_____

_____

_____

_____

_____

_____

_____

_____

_____

_____

_____

_____

Selection 1

Possible Student Responses

DAY 1: *Figurative language*

- The author uses the metaphor of the bee as "an honest citizen" who prefers "legitimate to illegitimate business." This personification creates interest in the reader and creates a sense of suspense in reference to the "hunt" and the "bee hunter."

- Students may have other answers that are certainly justified.

DAY 2: *Point of view/effective development*

- The author uses first person singular. This allows the speaker to become a hunter himself later in the paragraph.

DAY 3: *Word choice*

- Possible choices could include *fountain-head, stores, novice, wood-craft, exhilaration,* and so forth. What is most important is the student's selection of less-specific nouns and how they weaken the writing.

DAY 4: *Author's purpose/audience awareness*

- Students might assert that the author wrote this selection just to profess his love of nature or to explain the intricate behaviors of the bee. This selection might appear in a natural history magazine or collection of essays on nature.

- Students might be interested in knowing that John Burroughs was a naturalist who wrote the first biography of Walt Whitman. He wrote over twenty-nine books of essays and poetry.

DAY 5: *Analyzing writing*

- Most students will read this line as an extension of the metaphor. The rationales for students' answers are critical.

Selection 2

I Am From

[1] I am from hoops every night except Wednesday night,

[2] This is when the dealers come out to make a life.

[3] Where they sold in weather cold or hot,

[4] Some people dealed, and some people bought.

[5] I am from a hood park with a swing and a slide,

[6] To a neighborhood with a 2 story playset.

[7] Where the only neighborhood clubhouse is the cop trailer,

[8] To one with a big screen and a weight room.

[9] From a dirty basketball court by the road,

[10] To a lakeside one by the woods.

[11] I am from chain nets and square backboards,

[12] To new rims and nice courts.

[13] From one basketball with no grip,

[14] To one in every color with a built in pump.

[15] I am from cherishing my minor league baseball hat,

[16] To owning 10 fitted New Eras.

[17] From owning one generic football jersey,

[18] To owning a real one from every sport.

[19] I am from a school where the only sport to play was basketball,

(continued)

Selection 2

[20] To a school with sports I have never heard of.

[21] From a school that receives threats every three days and has a fight every two,

[22] To one that gets threats every three months and has a fight every few.

[23] I am from a city where mom made me stay on our block,

[24] To a city where not everyone has a lock.

[25] From a city where you had to work overtime to serve two,

[26] To a city when you can work anytime and call in with the flu.

[27] I am from a single parent household of three,

[28] And after marriage,

[29] The rest is history.

Meter and rhyme give poetry a regular, lyrical quality.

Selection 2

Daily Student Prompts

DAY 1

Why does the poet alternate the beginning of lines from "I am from" or "From" to "To (a)"?

DAY 2

Describe how the neighborhoods differ.

DAY 3

What evidence can you find that indicates that the speaker prefers one locale over the other?

DAY 4

Does this poem have a predictable rhyme scheme? Where does the poet use near or slant rhyme?

DAY 5

How does the final stanza differ from the other stanzas? How would you interpret "And after marriage/The rest is history"? Support your answers.

_____

_____

_____

_____

_____

_____

_____

_____

_____

_____

_____

_____

Selection 2

<u>*Possible Student Responses*</u>

DAY 1: *Poetry—form*

- The poet describes two places. The "I am from" lines refer to a previous neighborhood. Lines beginning with "To (a)" refer to his present neighborhood.

DAY 2: *Compare/contrast*

- Students may mention that the previous neighborhood had drug dealers, few pieces of recreation equipment, and police presence. He also describes his personal belongings: one cherished minor league hat before and ten expensive hats in his new neighborhood.

DAY 3: *Analyzing writing*

- Most students will defend that the speaker prefers his new home because of words/phrases such as "2 story playset," "big screen," "nice new rims," and so forth.

DAY 4: *Poetry—rhyme scheme*

- The first stanza seems to have a set pattern (aabb), but after that the pattern is irregular.

DAY 5: *Analyzing writing*

- Responses will vary. However, it is critical that students offer substantial support to justify their answers.

Selection 3

[1] Memories. [2] We all have them; we all endure them. [3] Songs have been sung about them, and people cry tears of joy over them. [4] However, by the time one gets to be quite old, one favorite memory will stand out above all the rest. [5] Be it that first kiss, your wedding day, or maybe even the day the kids moved away to college, one favorite memory will always endure.

[6] Memories are an important part of society today, as it can be seen by the avidity in which people preserve memories through photographs, video tapes, or even a diary. [7] Memories are heartwarming in that they let us relive our past wonderful experiences. [8] Memories are a time machine that whisk us away to the good times in life, as well as give us hope for the future that we will have more good memories.

[9] But, one favorite memory will always hold a special place in each of our hearts. [10] One thought of the past can bring us back to a time when we felt totally at peace with ourselves and the world. [11] It is important for us to be able to relive this moment, as it is a healing process to give us hope when we feel desolate.

[12] Even though memories are only in our minds and are not concrete, they still are an aspect of this life that gives it some meaning. [13] A favorite memory, however, is a magnification of this idea, and all of us have a favorite memory to endure.

Selection 3

Daily Student Prompts

DAY 1

The assignment for this essay was to write about a favorite memory. Did the author successfully complete the assignment? Defend your answer.

DAY 2

What is this essay's main weakness?

DAY 3

Correct the mechanical errors in sentence 3.

DAY 4

Sentence 2 also provides a strong thesis for this essay. Explain.

DAY 5

Write an introductory paragraph for your own memory essay; include a suitable title.

_____

_____

_____

_____

_____

_____

_____

_____

_____

_____

_____

_____

_____

_____

_____

Selection 3

<u>*Possible Student Responses*</u>

DAY 1: *Ideas/organization*

- This essay never addresses a specific memory. Rather, it addresses the topic of favorite memories.

DAY 2: *Ideas/organization*

- This essay has many weaknesses: organization, paragraph structure, and lack of specificity, to name a few. Support for answers is critical.

DAY 3: *Tense changes*

- Revisions will vary. Sample sentence:

    Songs have been sung about them, and people have cried tears of joy over them.

DAY 4: *Thesis*

- Sentence 2 offers the premise that memories are often *endured,* not necessarily *enjoyed.* The essay could focus on those endured memories and how they affect the speaker.

DAY 5: *Responding to a prompt*

- Introductions will vary.
- You may want to ask students to complete their essays.

Selection 4

Name
Address
Phone number
E-mail address

Objective:

Education:

Awards received:

Interests/activities:

Work experience:

Volunteer experience:

Honors:

Extracurricular activities:

Community activities:

References:

Selection 4

Daily Student Prompts

DAYS 1–5: Résumé/college application

Create a résumé that you can use for a job application, a college application, or even as a reference for individuals from whom you have requested a recommendation letter. Résumé formats vary, and this example can be modified to meet your needs.

Selection 4

<u>*Possible Student Responses*</u>

DAYS 1–5: *Résumé/college application*

- Sample résumé:

Jaime Hudson
100 Main St. Denver, CO 11111
555-555-1234
jaime@email.net

Objective: I am applying for admission to a four-year university.

Education: 2003–2007   Abraham Lincoln High School   Denver, CO

Awards received: Outstanding Science Award, 2004
Volunteer of the Year, 2005
Athlete/Scholar of the Year, 2006

Interests and activities: hockey, mountain climbing, archeology

Work experience: 2005–2007   Crew chief, Main St. Cafe, Denver, CO
Outstanding Employee, 2005 and 2006

Volunteer experience: Denver General Hospital, 2005–2006
Junior Hockey League, 2005–Present

Honors: National Honor Society, 2005–2007
Volunteer Honor Award, 2006 and 2007

Extracurricular activities: Varsity Hockey, 2005–2007
Interact Club, 2005–2007
Ski Club, 2006–2007

Community activities: Teen Court, 2006–2007

References: Available upon request

Selection 5

You will create the text for this week's selection.

DAY 1

_____   _____   _____
_____   _____   _____
_____   _____   _____
_____   _____   _____
_____   _____   _____
_____   _____   _____
_____   _____   _____

DAY 2

_____
_____
_____
_____
_____
_____
_____
_____
_____
_____

DAY 3

_____
_____
_____
_____
_____
_____
_____
_____
_____

(continued)

Selection 5

DAY 4

DAY 5

_____

_____

_____

_____

_____

_____

_____

_____

_____

_____

_____

_____

_____

_____

Selection 5

Daily Student Prompts

DAY 1

Make a list of fifteen to twenty words that you like. They might be words that have a unique sound, or you might just like the words' meanings. Think of songs you like, poems that appeal to you, or just draw the words from your experience.

DAY 2

Select a topic or subject, and write eight to ten sentences using your words from Day 1. Make sure you use at least one word from your list in each sentence. The sentences do not need to form a unified paragraph.

DAY 3

Select at least three of your sentences from Day 2 and develop them into one coherent paragraph. You may revise as needed.

DAY 4

Select at least eight to ten of your words from Day 1 and arrange them into a poem, beginning each line with a different selected word. Don't worry about rhyme or rhythm in this poem. If desired, just create phrases in a poem form.

DAY 5

Do one of the following: revise the paragraph from Day 3 into the first paragraph of a short story, or revise the poem you wrote yesterday.

Selection 5

Possible Student Responses

DAY 1: *Experimenting with language*

- You may need to help students begin generating their lists of words. You might list some of your favorite words and explain why they appeal to you.

DAY 2: *Experimenting with language*

- The writing exercises this week are meant to generate creative writing without creating strict boundaries for the students' writing. Encourage students to have fun with these exercises and not worry about their writing being "correct."

DAY 3: *Paragraph development*

- Stress paragraph continuity and structure to students as they create their paragraphs. Some students may think that stringing sentences together is all that is needed to write a paragraph. This is a good opportunity to review paragraph structure.

DAY 4: *Poetry*

- Again, encourage students to have fun with this exercise. They need not worry about the confines of rhyme or rhythm.

DAY 5: *Revision*

- Hopefully the writing from these exercises will produce some pieces that may be expanded and revised into substantial compositions.

Selection 6

¹ Going along the Appalachian Trail, you get all of the beauties that you could ask for in the way of majestic trees, wild flowers of various kinds at different times of the year. ² Going north from the southern end between Siler Bald and Clingmans Dome, the highest peak in the Smokies, you come across wood lilies, purple-fringed orchids, and all sorts of other wild Flowers. ³ Going on from Clingmans Dome to Newfound Gap, I remember one memorable trip under the leadership of Arthur Stupka, who was formerly the naturalist in the park. ⁴ All along the way from Indian Gap to Newfound Gap, during that late April day, we came across carpets of spring beauty—trout lily, trillium, and other wild flowers. ⁵ Then going on north from there, you strike other areas just as beautiful—witches hobble barely coming out at that time of year coming into full bloom later, then changing later still to the foliage that turns sometimes a yellow, sometimes bronze, like others of the viburnum family. ⁶ Then, of course, at different times of the year you run across trees in bloom—sarvis trees, as we call them, or service as they are otherwise called; silverbell; and later mountain ash. ⁷ Then, in their turn, the shrubs, like the red elderberry with its beautiful white blooms in the spring and then later on their brilliant red berries. ⁸ Then the various members of the heath family, like the azaleas and rhododendron, sand myrtle, and such a great variety of the wild flowers.

—A. Rufus Morgan,
Foxfire 4

Selection 6

Daily Student Prompts

DAY 1

How would you classify this writing? Part of a novel? Essay? Biography?

DAY 2

How is this paragraph structured?

DAY 3

As a reader, what type of background information would help you fully comprehend this paragraph?

DAY 4

What is the function of the semicolons in sentence 6?

DAY 5

Rewrite sentence 8, incorporating a semicolon that separates items in a series containing internal punctuation. You may add or delete words as necessary.

_____

_____

_____

_____

_____

_____

_____

_____

_____

_____

_____

_____

_____

_____

Selection 6

Possible Student Responses

DAY 1: *Genre*

- The writing is non-fiction, perhaps part of an expository essay or a biography.

DAY 2: *Organization*

- The paragraph begins with a clear topic sentence in sentence 1, followed by a series of supporting sentences. Also, this paragraph employs geographic organization as it describes the speaker's observations as he travels south to north.

DAY 3: *Analyzing writing/details*

- A reader unfamiliar with knowledge of this geographic area in the Smokies might have difficulty visualizing the descriptions. Also, knowledge of basic flowers and trees in the area would be helpful.

DAY 4: *Punctuation—semicolons*

- The semicolons separate items in a series containing internal punctuation.

DAY 5: *Punctuation—semicolons*

- There are many ways the sentence could be rewritten. Sample revision:
  Then there are various members of the heath family like the azaleas, always so vibrant; the rhododendron; the sand myrtle; and a great variety of the wild flowers.

Selection 7

Hurricane Isabel

2003-10-17, NASA photograph taken from *Expedition 7*

Writing that provides clear details and examples is more compelling than writing with vague, generic descriptions.

Selection 7

Daily Student Prompts

DAY 1

Write as many words or phrases as you can about the picture of Hurricane Isabel in five minutes. Don't worry about getting the "right" words; just create a list of impressions, thoughts, descriptions, and so forth.

DAY 2

Separate the words and phrases from the Day 1 list into two categories. Place the category name at the top of each list with the words and phrases beneath each category title. Create a third category for miscellaneous words that don't seem to fit in any other category, if necessary.

DAY 3

Select one category and expand five to eight words or phrases from that category into several sentences. You can modify the phrases as needed.

DAY 4

Organize the sentences from Day 3 into a logical sequence.

DAY 5

Revise your sentences from Day 4 into a coherent paragraph. Add and/or delete information or ideas as needed.

_____

_____

_____

_____

_____

_____

_____

_____

_____

_____

_____

_____

Selection 7

<u>*Possible Student Responses*</u>

DAY 1: *Generating effective ideas*

- This assignment lends itself to instructor participation. Encourage students to freely list any words that come to mind. They can eliminate unnecessary words later. You may want to preface the assignment with a discussion of the power and effects of hurricanes.

DAY 2: *Categorizing*

- Categorizing ideas and terms into lists often helps students organize ideas that can be used when writing paragraphs and essays. Creative writing assignments benefit from this technique as well.

DAY 3: *Generating effective ideas*

- Encourage students to expand words and phrases into sentences without worrying whether the sentences will "fit together." Students can freely revise and edit on Day 4.

DAY 4: *Organization*

- This assignment may be the most difficult for students. You may wish to have students develop a topic sentence, and then organize their sentences to coordinate with the topic sentence.

DAY 5: *Revision*

- You may want to ask students to expand their paragraphs into longer pieces of writing. If you have participated in this week's exercises, students will enjoy seeing your finished product.

Selection 8

1. Injustice is relatively easy to bear what stings is justice (H.L. Menken)

2. Most businesses in our country agree that international trade is mandatory few could survive without it

3. Soccer is quickly becoming a major sport in America, this is evident from the large number of youth soccer leagues in our country

4. Hydrogen cars offer a solution for our country's energy crisis however there are complications to making a smooth transition to mass consumption of hydrogen power

5. Animated films are now accepted as a substantial part of Hollywood filmmaking Cars for instance is an example of a successful and profitable Hollywood animated film

6. Choosing a college or technical school is a difficult process for most high school students and many students will transfer to other schools after they attend an institution for just one year

7. Many teenagers hold part-time jobs as clerks salespersons often in retail malls fast-food cooks and babysitters

8. Unless you carefully select an institution of higher learning you might find that you will lose money and time attending a school that does not fit your needs

9. Many diets limit the intake of the following sugar foods high in cholesterol processed foods soda and caffeine

10. Minds are like parachutes They function only when open

Selection 8

Daily Student Prompts

DAY 1

Copy and correctly punctuate sentences 1 and 2. Make sure you punctuate so that each number remains a single sentence; do not delete or add any words.

DAY 2

Copy and correctly punctuate sentences 3 and 4. Make sure you punctuate so that each number remains a single sentence; do not delete or add any words.

DAY 3

Copy and correctly punctuate sentences 5 and 6. Make sure you punctuate so that each number remains a single sentence; do not delete or add any words.

DAY 4

Copy and correctly punctuate sentences 7 and 8. Make sure you punctuate so that each number remains a single sentence; do not delete or add any words.

DAY 5

Copy and correctly punctuate sentences 9 and 10. Make sure you punctuate so that each number remains a single sentence; do not delete or add any words.

_____

_____

_____

_____

_____

_____

_____

_____

_____

_____

_____

_____

_____

Selection 8

Possible Student Responses

DAY 1: *Punctuation—period, semicolon*

1. Injustice is relatively easy to bear; what stings is justice.

2. Most businesses in our country agree that international trade is mandatory; few could survive without it.

- One use of the semicolon is to connect independent clauses which are related but not connected by a coordinating conjunction.

DAY 2: *Punctuation—comma, period, semicolon*

3. Soccer is quickly becoming a major sport in America; this is evident from the large number of youth soccer leagues in our country.

4. Hydrogen cars offer a solution for our country's energy crisis; however, there are complications to making a smooth transition to the mass consumption of hydrogen power.

- Sentence 3 corrects the comma splice error in the original sentence. Sentence 4 contains two independent clauses connected with a transitional term. Point out to students that the semicolon appears before the transitional term if it initiates the second independent clause.

DAY 3: *Punctuation—comma, period, semicolon*

5. Animated films are now accepted as a substantial part of Hollywood filmmaking; Cars, for instance, is an example of a successful and profitable animated Hollywood film.

6. Choosing a college or technical school is a difficult process for most high school students, and many students will transfer to other schools after they attend an institution for just one year.

- Sentence 5 is an example of a sentence with two independent clauses and a transitional term in the middle of the second clause. In this case, the transitional term is set off with commas.

- Because sentence 6 contains a coordinating conjunction between the two independent clauses, no semicolon is needed. A comma is required before the coordinating conjunction.

(continued)

Selection 8

DAY 4: *Punctuation—comma, period, semicolon*

7. Many teenagers hold part-time jobs as clerks; salespersons, often in retail malls; fast-food cooks; and babysitters.

8. Unless you carefully select an institution of higher learning, you might find that you will lose money and time attending a school that does not fit your needs.

- Sentence 7 contains a series with internal punctuation and thereby requires semicolons to separate each element of the series.

- Sentence 8 contains a subordinating clause and an independent clause and therefore requires a comma after the subordinating clause, not a semicolon.

DAY 5: *Punctuation—comma, period, colon*

9. Many diets limit the intake of the following: sugar, foods high in cholesterol, processed foods, soda, and caffeine.

10. Minds are like parachutes: They function only when open.

- Sentence 9 needs a colon after the initial independent clause to introduce a list. Note that some eliminate the comma between the last two elements in a list.

- Sentence 10 needs a colon to separate independent clauses because the second clause summarizes the first clause. In this case, the second independent clause may begin with a capital letter or a lowercase letter.

Selection 9

The essay below was written in response to the following prompt:

A law has been passed changing the state's driver's license system to a graduated system. A restricted license will be issued to qualified sixteen-year-old drivers, and an unrestricted license will be issued to qualified seventeen-year-old drivers. Argue for or against this system.

[1] A law has been passed changing the driver's license system to a graduated system. [2] I support passing this law. [3] This system has the chance of keeping young driver's safe. [4] Limiting the number of passengers and limiting the time teenagers can drive <u>gives him or her more time to get use to driving</u>. [5] The full license at age 17 is the best age.

[6] First, at 15 most kids aren't grown up enough to drive and be responsible, some teenagers would take advantage of a privilege such as driving to show off to friends. [7] A teenager like this should receive a restricted learner's license. [8] By having an adult drive with them and not a lot of friends in the car can help them focus on their surroundings. [9] Distractions cause a lot of accidents.

[10] Second, a 16 year old might have a job and they complain that they shouldn't have restricted hours so they can work. [11] This is totally wrong. [12] They shouldn't be working late at night anyway. [13] And by driving late when you are just starting to drive is asking for trouble. [14] If someone would fall asleep at the wheel after a long day, that would be terrible. [15] Especially at such a young age. [16] This is the reason 16 is a good reason for a restricted license.

[17] Third, when a teenager is 17, they are probably fixing to graduate from high school and are mature enough to be careful when driving. [18] They are more likely not to show off and keep themselves from being distracted.

[19] This new law will keep teenage drivers safe. [20] You should agree with this new law. [21] It was passed to keep teenagers from dying. [22] By giving teenagers time to learn to drive without distractions is the way people should learn to drive.

Selection 9

Daily Student Prompts

DAY 1

The author of this essay presents three arguments in support of the new driving law. Identify which argument you think is strongest. Defend your answer.

DAY 2

Review the underlined section of sentence 4, and select a revision (if needed) from the following:

    a. no change

    b. has given him more time to get used to driving

    c. gives him or her more time to get use to driving

    d. give them more time to get used to driving

DAY 3

The last sentence of paragraph 2 makes an assertion without offering any support. What might the author have added to this paragraph to strengthen the paragraph and justify the assertion?

DAY 4

The introductory terms (first, second, third) in paragraphs 2, 3, and 4 are rather mundane and weaken this paper. Revise and strengthen the beginning sentences in these three paragraphs.

DAY 5

The final paragraph of this essay is disorganized and weakens the overall argument. Rewrite a stronger concluding paragraph for this essay.

_____

_____

_____

_____

_____

_____

_____

_____

Selection 9

<u>*Possible Student Responses*</u>

DAY 1: *Ideas/supporting details*

- Students might identify an argument that has widespread appeal to adults and teenagers. They might evaluate an argument based on the logic of the argument or the strength of the author's support.

DAY 2: *Subject/verb agreement—pronoun/antecedent agreement*

- There is a plural subject in this sentence and a singular verb.

- The original sentence has a pronoun/antecedent error: *teenagers* (pl.) and the verb *gives* (sing.).

- There is also an idiomatic error: *to get use to.*

- Answer *d* is correct.

DAY 3: *Supporting details*

- One of the main weaknesses of a persuasive or argumentative essay is the presence of assertions without supporting evidence. Students might give statistics of accidents caused by cell phone use or perhaps relate examples of fellow students who have been in accidents caused by the distractions of teen passengers.

DAY 4: *Transitions*

- Strong transitions give the reader a signal that makes connections between ideas. Stronger transitions might include "For example" for paragraph 2, "Even though" for paragraph 3, and "Moreover" for paragraph 4.

DAY 5: *Effective conclusion*

- Responses will vary.

- A stronger conclusion might include a plea for teens to comply with the new law for the sake of themselves and their passengers.

Selection 10

No selection is needed for this week's workout.

Daily Student Prompts

DAY 1

Write 100 words (in sentences) on a single topic of your choice. Select a topic that is important to you or about which you have significant knowledge.

DAY 2

Change all the verbs from Day 1 into the past tense. Look carefully and strengthen weak or vague verbs with specific, active verbs.

DAY 3

Expand your 100 words with a memory from your past about your selected topic. Make sure you include enough specific description that the reader will be able to understand your memory.

DAY 4

Infuse an emotion into the writing you have created this week. You may revise and/or add words, phrases, and sentences as you choose.

DAY 5

Infuse a place or locale into the writing you have created this week. Revise your writing from this week and make any necessary corrections so that your work is coherent and clear. Then, add one last sentence at the end of your selection that makes a strong impact on the reader. Share your writing with another classmate.

_____

_____

_____

_____

_____

_____

_____

_____

_____

Selection 10

Possible Student Responses

DAY 1: *Generating effective ideas*

- A few minutes of prewriting discussion may facilitate student writing for this assignment.

DAY 2: *Tense changes*

- A quick review of past tense may be required for this assignment.

DAY 3: *Generating effective ideas*

- Students may need to expand their writing from the original 100 words.

DAY 4: *Tone/revision*

- Beginning today's assignment with brainstorming a list of emotions may help students complete the assignment.

DAY 5: *Setting/revision*

- Students may equate shock with impact. Sharing this week's writing may help students understand the difference.

Selection 11

Principal Parts of Verbs

Present: love   Past: loved   Past participle: loved   Infinitive: to love

Indicative mood: present tense		
	Singular	Plural
1st person	I love	we love
2nd person	you love	you love
3rd person	he loves	they love

Indicative mood: present perfect tense		
	Singular	Plural
1st person	I have loved	we have loved
2nd person	you have loved	you have loved
3rd person	she had loved	they have loved

Indicative mood: past tense		
	Singular	Plural
1st person	I loved	we loved
2nd person	you loved	you loved
3rd person	she loved	they loved

Indicative mood: past perfect tense		
	Singular	Plural
1st person	I had loved	we had loved
2nd person	you had loved	you had loved
3rd person	he had loved	they had loved

Indicative mood: future tense		
	Singular	Plural
1st person	I will love	they will love
2nd person	you will love	you will love
3rd person	he will love	they will love

Indicative mood: future perfect tense		
	Singular	Plural
1st person	I will have loved	we will have loved
2nd person	you will have loved	you will have loved
3rd person	she will have loved	they will have loved

Selection 11

Daily Student Prompts

DAY 1

Select an active verb that you will use for this week's exercises.

Write the present, past, and past participle of your verb.

Write a sentence using your verb in the present perfect tense, third person plural.

DAY 2

Conjugate your verb in the past tense, singular and plural.

Write a sentence using your verb in the second person plural, future tense.

DAY 3

Write a sentence using your verb in the third person singular, present perfect tense. When does this action take place?

DAY 4

Write a sentence using your verb in the first person singular, past perfect tense. When does this action take place?

DAY 5

Write a sentence using your verb in the first person singular, future perfect tense. When does this action take place?

_____

_____

_____

_____

_____

_____

_____

_____

_____

_____

_____

Selection 11

Possible Student Responses

DAY 1: *Tense changes*

- Some students may be unfamiliar with the terms *mood* and *tense.* A quick review of indicative mood (facts, opinions, and questions), imperative mood (orders), and subjunctive (wishes or conditions) might be helpful. Explain that tense refers to the time of an event as related to when the author writes about the event. Shifting tenses is often a common occurrence in students' writing, but without knowledge of the tenses, they do not know how to rectify this problem.

DAY 2: *Tense changes*

- Again, some students will not be familiar with the term *conjugate.* Using the samples from Selection 11 will clarify the term for them.

DAY 3: *Tense changes*

- Many students will not know that present perfect tense indicates action that began in the past and is still occurring in the present.

DAY 4: *Tense changes*

- Many students will not know that past perfect tense indicates action that has been completed by the time another act in the past takes place.

DAY 5: *Tense changes*

- Many students will not know that future perfect tense is used when an action will have been completed before or by a certain future date.

Selection 12

1. having been poor is no shame but being ashamed of it is said benjamin franklin

2. ben franklin said genius without education is like silver in the mine

3. a slip of the foot you may soon recover benjamin franklin said but a slip of the tongue you may never get over

4. mama sent me too. when my sister Sonya was sending me mama also came over and said run quickly polenka (*Crime and Punishment*, Fyodor Dostoevsky)

5. i beg your pardon captain he began quite casually suddenly addressing nikodim fomich but you must also understand my position (*Crime and Punishment*, Fyodor Dostoevsky)

6. mrs westons manners said emma were always particularly good their propriety simplicity and elegance would make them the safest model for any young woman (*Emma*, Jane Austen)

7. mr perry said he in a voice of very strong displeasure would do as well to keep his opinion till it is asked for why does he make it any business of his to wonder at what I do (*Emma*, Jane Austen)

8. monseigneur hear me monseigneur hear my petition my husband died of want so many die of want so many more will die of want (*A Tale of Two Cities*, Charles Dickens)

9. i want said defarge who had not removed is gaze from the shoemaker to let in a little more light here you can bear a little more (*A Tale of Two Cities*, Charles Dickens)

Selection 12

Daily Student Prompts

DAY 1

Correctly rewrite and edit sentences 1, 2, and 3.

DAY 2

Rewrite sentence 4 with a quote within a quote; include correct punctuation as needed.

Edit sentence 5. (This sentence contains a quotation and a direct address.)

DAY 3

Rewrite and edit sentences 6 and 7.

DAY 4

Rewrite and edit sentences 8 (three sentences) and 9 (two sentences) with quotation marks and other corrections as needed.

DAY 5

List other uses of quotation marks in addition to indicating direct and indirect quotations.

Selection 12

Possible Student Responses

DAY 1: *Punctuation—quotation marks, commas, periods/capitalization*

1. "Having been poor is no shame, but being ashamed of it, is," said Benjamin Franklin.

2. Ben Franklin said, "Genius without education is like silver in the mine."

3. "A slip of the foot you may soon recover," Benjamin Franklin said, "but a slip of the tongue you may never get over."

DAY 2: *Punctuation—quotation marks, commas, periods/capitalization*

4. "Mama sent me too. When my sister Sonya was sending me, mama also came over and said, 'Run quickly, Polenka.' "

5. "I beg your pardon, Captain," he began quite casually, suddenly addressing Nikodim Fomich, "but you must also understand my position."

DAY 3: *Punctuation—quotation marks, apostrophes, commas, periods/capitalization*

6. "Mrs. Weston's manners," said Emma, "were always particularly good. Their propriety, simplicity, and elegance would make them the safest model for any young woman."

7. "Mr. Perry," said he, in a voice of very strong displeasure, "would do as well to keep his opinion till it is asked for. "Why does he make it any business of his to wonder at what I do?"

DAY 4: *Punctuation—quotation marks, semicolons, commas, end punctuation*

8. "Monseigneur, hear me! Monseigneur, hear my petition! My husband died of want; so many die of want; so many more will die of want."

9. "I want," said Defarge, who had not removed is gaze from the shoemaker, "to let in a little more light here. You can bear a little more?" (The final sentence can be written as a statement.)

DAY 5: *Punctuation—quotation marks*

• Students might list using quotation marks to indicate titles of articles in newspapers and magazines; and titles of short poems, short stories, songs, and chapters.

Selection 13

This exercise requires a postcard or a piece of paper the size of a postcard.

Daily Student Prompts

DAYS 1–4

You are to create a short story that will fit on a postcard. You should spend the beginning of the week deciding on a setting, creating characters, and developing a plot. Needless to say, you must carefully refine and focus your ideas. You may use both sides of the postcard, but you must complete the story using only the postcard (or a piece of paper the size of a postcard).

DAY 5

Today you are to make any last-minute revisions and then copy your final story on the postcard. If time permits, share your story with the class.

_____

_____

_____

_____

_____

_____

_____

_____

_____

_____

_____

_____

_____

_____

_____

_____

Selection 13

Possible Student Responses

DAYS 1–5: *Generating effective, clear ideas/effective organization*

- Students should find this exercise enjoyable and challenging. Paring down a story to fit on a postcard forces students to progress quickly from a conflict to a climax, then clearly develop a resolution. During the week, you might discuss what the students had to sacrifice in order to fit their stories into such a confined space. Was the plot compromised? Was it at all possible to develop characters? Sharing the short, short stories with the class may provide a welcome end-of-the-week activity. You might inform students that there are numerous short, short story contests that they might like to enter. A search of the Internet will give them more information concerning these contests.

Selection 14

Dear Fellow Freshman,

[1] Three years ago, I was in the same situation as you are in now. [2] I was clueless and essentially overwhelmed. [3] I was a new student in high school who did not know the teachers, many students, and I didn't know how the system worked. [4] Learn from my experiences, freshman and you'll be just fine.

[5] The most important lesson I learned was to be a head of the teachers, actually just be prepared. [6] If you do your work on time, the teachers are much less grouchy. [7] Trust me on that one! [8] You might even pass your classes. [9] That makes your parents much less grouchy. [10] Trust me on that one too.

[11] Now I know the best part about school is talking to you're friends, not the classes. [12] However, if your late to class to often, there is this detention room that will become your home away from home if your not carefull. [13] Again, this is experience talking here. [14] You don't want to spent even a day with the detention superviser; I think his previous job was a guard in a maxemum security prison. [15] He has no sense of humor; again I know this from experience.

[16] About the teachers—

When the parts of a sentence are not in order or if the punctuation is incorrect, the meaning of the sentence will be unclear.

Selection 14

Daily Student Prompts

DAY 1

Copy sentences 1 and 2 and combine them into one sentence.

Revise sentence 3 beginning with "As a new student."

DAY 2

What grammatical error(s) exist in sentence 4?

Combine sentences 9 and 10 into one sentence.

DAY 3

Find and correct any spelling errors in paragraph 3 (sentences 11 through 15).

DAY 4

In the same tone as the rest of this letter, write paragraph 4 about your experiences with teachers during your freshman year.

DAY 5

Write a concluding paragraph for this letter, and include any last pieces of advice for an incoming freshman.

_____

_____

_____

_____

_____

_____

_____

_____

_____

_____

_____

_____

_____

Selection 14

Possible Student Responses

DAY 1: *Sentence combining*

- One possible combination is: Three years ago, I was in the same situation as you are in now; I was clueless and overwhelmed. (This is a good opportunity to review the semicolon.)

- One possible revision for sentence 3 is: As a new student in high school, I did not know the teachers, many students, or how the system worked.

DAY 2: *Sentence combining/punctuation—commas*

- "Freshman" should be set off with commas—direct address.

- One possible combination for sentences 9 and 10: That makes your parents much less grouchy, and you can trust me on that one, too. Students might combine the sentences using a semicolon.

DAY 3: *Spelling*

- Sentence 11: your
- Sentence 12: you're, too, you're, careful
- Sentence 14: spend, supervisor, maximum
- You might assign students to revise and edit paragraph 3 rather than just correct the spelling.

DAY 4: *Responding to a prompt/tone*

- Students may enjoy sharing their paragraphs with the class.

DAY 5: *Effective conclusion*

- This is a good writing assignment for graduating seniors. You might share the letters with teachers who will teach incoming freshmen the next year.

Selection 15

1. I (accept, except) your apology, but you still hurt my feelings.

2. My guidance counselor's (advise, advice) was to apply to several colleges instead of just one.

3. I've (already, all ready) promised to go to Homecoming with someone else.

4. The (amount, number) of workers at the construction site is incredible.

5. I am so (angry at, angry with) Yuko.

6. (Anyone, any one) who wants to come to the lake with us should meet at Emma's at 2 P.M.

7. (Beside, Besides) Claire, Clark is also allergic to peanuts.

8. Please (bring, take) the calculator to my office on your way home.

9. You must be careful when you (cite, site) sources in your research paper.

10. Antonio's (conscious, conscience) bothered him all night after he offended his friend.

11. I (could of, could have) danced another hour if the band hadn't stopped playing.

12. Only the legislature can (affect, effect) a major change in foreign policy.

13. The (council, counsel) for the defense asked for an adjournment.

14. I'm (disinterested, uninterested) in your obsession with ice hockey.

15. I don't want to (differ from, differ with) you, but you're just not being rational.

Selection 15

Daily Student Prompts
DAY 1
Select the correct word or phrase for sentences 1, 2, and 3.
DAY 2
Select the correct word or phrase for sentences 4, 5, and 6.
DAY 3
Select the correct word or phrase for sentences 7, 8, and 9.
DAY 4
Select the correct word or phrase for sentences 10, 11, and 12.
DAY 5
Select the correct word or phrase for sentences 13, 14, and 15.

_____

_____

_____

_____

_____

_____

_____

_____

_____

_____

_____

_____

_____

_____

_____

_____

_____

_____

Selection 15

Possible Student Responses

DAY 1: *Usage*

1. accept

   Accept means "to receive," and *except* usually means "excluding."

2. advice

   Advice is a noun; *advise* is a verb.

3. already

   Already means "previously," and *all ready* means "prepared."

DAY 2: *Usage*

4. number

   Number is used with quantities that can be counted; *amount* is used with quantities that cannot be counted.

5. angry with

   Angry at is not standard usage.

6. Anyone

   Anyone is an indefinite pronoun; *any one* is comprised of the adjective *any* and the pronoun *one* and refers to a specific element in a group.

DAY 3: *Usage*

7. Besides

   Beside is a preposition that means "next to;" *besides* is a preposition that means "except."

8. bring

   Bring refers to moving an object toward someone; *take* refers to moving an object away.

9. cite

   Cite is to quote as an example; *site* is a noun meaning "a specific place."

(continued)

Selection 15

DAY 4: *Usage*

10. conscience

    Conscience is a noun that refers to the awareness of a moral principle; *conscious* is an adjective meaning "aware."

11. could have

    Could of is not standard usage.

12. effect

    In this case, *effect* is used as a verb meaning "to bring about." Often, *effect* is a noun meaning "result," and *affect* is a verb meaning "to influence."

DAY 5: *Usage*

13. counsel

    Counsel can mean "advice" or "lawyer." A *council* is an assembly or body of law.

14. uninterested

    Uninterested means "not interested;" *disinterested* means "objective."

15. differ with

    Differ with means "to disagree;" *differ from* means "to be unlike."

Selection 16

Select a short story or a portion of a novel that you have read in class this year or have read in the past. You will need a copy of the text for the rest of the week's assignments.

Daily Student Prompts

DAYS 1–4

Your assignment this week is to rewrite a scene from your short story or novel from the perspective of a character other than from whom it was originally presented. For example, you could rewrite the scene where the girls look for snacks in "A & P" from the perspective of one of the girls. Perhaps you could rewrite the fight scene from "Battle Royal" by Ralph Ellison from the speaker's grandfather's perspective. You should complete this assignment by Day 4 so you can share your work on Day 5.

DAY 5

Share your rewritten scene with a partner or the entire class. You may need to review the original perspective if your partner or class is not familiar with your selection.

Selection 16

Possible Student Responses

DAYS 1–4: *Responding to a prompt/revision*

- This assignment can be structured in various ways. If the class has read a common selection, you might wish to assign the selection. You might choose to have students select partners on Day 1 and assign each partner to use the same selection. This is a challenging assignment, but most students enjoy writing the revised scene.

DAY 5: *Sharing*

- Students will share their revision with a partner, small group, or the entire class, as desired.

Selection 17

[1] I heartily accept the motto, "That government is best which governs least; and I should like to see it acted up to more rapidly and systematically. [2] Carried out, it finally amounts to this, which also I believe—"That government is best which governs not at all"; and when men are prepared for it, that will be the kind of government which they will have. [3] Government is at best but an expedient; but most governments are usually, and all governments are sometimes, inexpedient. [4] The objections which have been brought against a standing army, and they are many and weighty, and deserve to prevail, may also at last be brought against a standing government. [5] The standing army is only an arm of the standing government. [6] The government itself, which is only the mode which the people have chosen to execute their will, is equally liable to be abused and perverted before the people can act through it. [7] Witness the present Mexican war, the work of comparatively a few individuals using the standing government as their tool; for in the outset, the people would not have consented to this measure.

—"Civil Disobedience" by Henry David Thoreau, 1849

Good writers state the main idea early on in the essay and support the statement with details.

Selection 17

Daily Student Prompts

DAY 1

This week you will be paraphrasing a portion of Thoreau's "Civil Disobedience." Paraphrasing is an extremely useful tool when trying to comprehend complicated text. Unlike summarizing, paraphrasing requires word-for-word or phrase-by-phrase rewording of an author's words, and is often longer than the original text. You should attempt to include all of the author's ideas and present these ideas objectively (and not include your opinion of the author's ideas). The sentences will be yours, but the ideas will be Thoreau's. As you will soon understand, this process is time-consuming and difficult to use with long texts.

Here are some guidelines to use when paraphrasing:

- Initially read and reread the original passage until you are very familiar with it.
- Look up any unfamiliar words in the dictionary and note the definitions.
- Make note of any quotations you may wish to include in the paraphrase. (An author's exact words always must be enclosed in quotation marks.)
- Translate the selection into your words, making sure that you explain anything that is critical to comprehending the piece.

Practice paraphrasing with the following sentence from "Civil Disobedience."

He who gives himself entirely to his fellow men appears to them useless and selfish; but he who gives himself partially to them is pronounced a benefactor and philanthropist.

DAY 2

Paraphrase sentences 1 and 2 from the "Civil Disobedience" excerpt.

DAY 3

Paraphrase sentences 3 and 4 from the "Civil Disobedience" excerpt.

DAY 4

Paraphrase sentences 5 and 6 from the "Civil Disobedience" excerpt.

DAY 5

Paraphrase sentence 7 from the "Civil Disobedience" excerpt. Reread your paraphrase, and revise your work as needed.

Selection 17

<u>*Possible Student Responses*</u>

DAY 1: *Paraphrasing*

- This is a difficult assignment, and often students summarize rather than paraphrase. Today's assignment, therefore, is crucial. You might wish to paraphrase the sample sentence as a whole-class assignment.

- A possible paraphrasing of the sample sentence is: A person who dedicates his entire life to others, and does not maintain a personal identity, or ego, may seem weak and ineffective to other people. But if a person retains a sense of self, of ego, and then dedicates a portion of his life to others, he may ironically seem to be more giving and generous than the person who professes complete dedication to others.

DAYS 2–5: *Paraphrasing/revision*

- Students will need access to dictionaries for this assignment and may need your assistance as well. This exercise gives students a method of dealing with complicated text. Having students share their paraphrases with the class might be valuable. You might discuss whether this assignment would produce different paraphrases if the assignment had been made in a history or government class. Also, it would be interesting to have a history or government teacher complete the paraphrasing and share that writing with the class on Day 5.

Selection 18

[1] "Experience is the best teacher" to me means that people who have more life experiences are usually more intelligent and more tuned in to life. [2] He often knows more about life and how to deal with them. [3] I have learned alot from some experiences and they have opened my mind to new ideas. [4] Because of that, I have been able to teach from them.

[5] One thing that taught me was when a friend of mine was hurt in a car accident. [6] He was a close friend of mine and I was crushed when I heard he was in the hospital. [7] We had met at the rec center a few years earlier and had become good friends. [8] At first I was mad at Jorge because he was speeding but then I realized I just needed to be a good friend to him. [9] After he got out of the hospital, we talked for hours. [10] I learned that good friends are few and far between.

[11] Another lesson I had was when my dog was killed by a car in front of our house. [12] My dad was always on me to latch the front screen door because Ralphy (our border collie) could open the screen door if the latch wasn't hooked. [13] I had come in from school in a bad mood because I had failed my algebra test. [14] I didn't latch the screen door, I now admit. [15] When Ralphy heard some kids playing in the street, he rushed out to play with them and was hit by a car. [16] That was a hard lesson to learn because I loved that dog so much.

[17] The more experiences you have, the smarter you get. [18] I think I know what that means now but I didn't know what it meant a few years ago. [19] If you don't believe me, you will in the future because the more experiences you have, the better off you will be because of your experiences.

Selection 18

DAY 1

The objective of this essay is to convince someone that "experience is the best teacher." Do you agree with the author's thesis statement in sentence one? Defend your answer. Explain what is weak or effective about the author's statement. Correct the mechanical and grammatical errors in paragraph 1.

DAY 2

Identify the topic sentence in paragraph 2. Does the writer effectively support this statement? Is it appropriate to place the topic sentence where it is located in the paragraph? Rewrite sentence ten, omitting the cliché "few and far between."

DAY 3

What is the main idea of paragraph 3? Is this stated explicitly or implied? What is the advantage of implying a main idea over stating it explicitly?

DAY 4

How does the writer organize this essay? Identify another way of organizing this essay.

DAY 5

The concluding paragraph is very weak. Rewrite a conclusion for this selection.

_____

_____

_____

_____

_____

_____

_____

_____

_____

_____

_____

_____

Selection 18

Possible Student Responses

DAY 1: *Argumentation, analyzing writing, pronoun/antecedent*

- Most students will agree that experience is a good teacher, but they may take issue with the author's statement that experience makes one more intelligent or more "tuned in to life."

- Errors include the following:

   pronoun/antecedent error in sentence 2 ("He" and "them"), "alot" in sentence 3, "teach" instead of "learn" in sentence 4

   This paragraph remains weak even after correcting the mechanical errors.

DAY 2: *Main idea/supporting details*

- The main idea of "good friends are few and far between" is not sufficiently supported in this paragraph. A class discussion of a more appropriate topic sentence may be helpful. Also, many students believe that a topic sentence must appear at the beginning of a paragraph. A discussion of the effect of placing the statement at the end of a paragraph might enlighten some readers to the power of this technique.

DAY 3: *Main idea*

- Some students might believe that an implied main idea statement weakens an essay. Remind students that if a writer uses an implied main idea, there must be sufficient and unified support. If students think the main idea of the paragraph is to latch the screen door, they have missed the larger issue of responsibility.

DAY 4: *Organization*

- The organization of this essay is very predictable and indicative of one prepared for a standardized writing assessment. Varying introductory sentences, strengthening (or adding) transitions, and elaborating more clearly are a few ways to improve this piece.

DAY 5: *Effective conclusion/revision*

- Revisions must unify this paragraph. The existing concluding paragraph is shallow and essentially meaningless.

Selection 19

1. I'm afraid that a time tested remedy will not work in this case.

2. The district attorney was merciless when she cross examined the defendant.

3. Would you like front, middle, or center-row tickets?

4. Dr. Elliot is a well respected physician.

5. One fifth of the students in my calculus class failed the test.

6. Self help books have become incredibly popular in the past few years.

7. Antiintellectualism surged when the militant government seized power.

8. I am hesitant really hesitant to sign this contract.

9. The cost of basic goods food shelter fuel remain a major concern to most Americans.

10. There were various reasons for the uprising   even though the primary cause was not evident.

11. Three new members of the Green Party announced their candidacy.   Additional candidates from the other parties are expected to make announcements tomorrow.

12. Jack and Jill went up the hill to fetch a pail of water

    And Jill came tumbling after.

13. The defense attorney criticized district attorney larson for including mason electronics in the class action suit.

14. The president was elected to a six year term beginning in march.

15. When the federal bureau of investigation asked for additional assistance extra investigators ground support and technical expertise the response was swift and substantial.

Selection 19

DAY 1

Correct any errors in sentences 1 through 3.

DAY 2

Correct any errors in sentences 4 through 6.

DAY 3

Correct any errors in sentences 7 through 9.

DAY 4

Correctly punctuate sentences 10 through 12; a blank space in a sentence indicates omitted words or sentences.

DAY 5

Correct any errors in sentences 13 through 15.

Selection 19

<u>*Possible Student Responses*</u>

DAY 1: *Punctuation—hyphens*

1.   I'm afraid that a time-tested remedy will not work in this case.

2.   The district attorney was merciless when she cross-examined the defendant.

3.   Would you like front-, middle-, or center-row tickets?

DAY 2: *Punctuation—hyphens*

4.   Dr. Elliot is a well-respected physician.

5.   One-fifth of the students in my calculus class failed the test.

6.   Self-help books have become incredibly popular in the past few years.

DAY 3: *Punctuation—hyphens, dashes*

7.   Anti-intellectualism surged when the militant government seized power.

8.   I am hesitant—really hesitant—to sign this contract.

9.   The cost of basic goods—food, shelter, and fuel—remain a major concern to most Americans.

Remind students that the dash is created by using two hyphens and sets off parenthetical material that deserves emphasis. It is also used to set off an appositive that contains commas.

(continued)

Selection 19

DAY 4: *Punctuation—ellipsis*

If students arc not familiar with the use of ellipses, a short review might be necessary before completing today's assignment.

10. "There were various reasons for the uprising . . . even though the primary cause was not evident."

11. "Three new members of the Green Party announced their candidacy. . . . Additional candidates from the other parties are expected to make announcements tomorrow."

12. Jack and Jill went up the hill to fetch a pail of water

    . . . .

    And Jill came tumbling after.

    (When skipping a line of poetry, the writer uses a full line of dots to indicate the omission.)

DAY 5: *Capitalization/punctuation—hyphens, dashes*

13. The defense attorney criticized District Attorney Larson for including Mason Electronics in the class-action suit.

14. The president was elected to a six-year term beginning in March.

15. When the Federal Bureau of Investigation asked for additional assistance—extra investigators, ground support, and technical expertise—the response was swift and substantial.

Selection 20

[1] Anyway, we lived there, and we went from one sawmill camp to another. [2] That was the only business there was in Rabun County—sawmills. [3] My dad made a dollar a day working at the sawmill. [4] You didn't get money. [5] You got to order it [in credit] at the store, and you'd take that and get whatever groceries you needed, or whatever you had to have. [6] And if you needed shoes, it was the same way. [7] So we got one pair a year, and if you wore them out in the wintertime, you didn't need any in the summer. [8] That was it. [9] I used to tote wood and go with my feet wrapped up with a sack on top of my shoe.

[10] When we moved over here at the head of Timpson Creek, I started to school. [11] I was seven years old. [12] I went to first grade up here at Clayton and made it fine. [13] We rode an old bus—an A Model Ford that had a homemade hickey [carriage] on it. [14] You know, they didn't build 'em then like they do now. [15] That was the hardest riding thing that ever was. [16] The second year, at Christmastime, the teachers in the state of Georgia hadn't been paid in six months, so families had to pay two dollars and a half a month for each student—or go home. [17] I went home.

[18] After that we moved to Germany [Mountain, near Clayton] and farmed. [19] Of course, most people farmed back then. [20] That was about all you could do to keep from starving to death. [21] We lived on Mr. Bynum's farm. [22] He had two old steers, and that was what we made a crop with—animals. [23] And that's "some fun" plowing them things. [24] Me and my daddy hewed cross ties with an ax in the wintertime, and we'd bring 'em [by oxen] to Clayton on Saturday to sell 'em. I guess it's about ten or twelve miles, and it would take us from daylight that morning till ten o'clock that night to take them slow things [steers] to Clayton and back. [25] And we'd sell the cross ties and buy groceries.

—Melvin Taylor, *The Foxfire Book*

Selection 20

Daily Student Prompts

Form a writing-response group according to your teacher's instructions. Each day you will analyze the selection from *The Foxfire Book*. *The Foxfire Books* were compiled by high school students in Rabun County, Georgia, in the sixties and seventies. The objective of the books was to document and preserve the students' mountain heritage. Currently, 8.5 million copies of *The Foxfire Books* have been published; twelve separate volumes are available.

DAY 1

What is this author's main point? Who is the intended audience?

DAY 2

Sentences 8 and 17 are extremely short. What is the effect of including such short sentences in this selection?

What is the function of the brackets in sentences 13, 18, and 24?

Is this selection well organized? Defend your answers.

DAY 3

What specific evidence does the author present that helps the reader understand the Depression?

What statements or phrases evoke a strong response from you? Why?

DAY 4

In order to completely understand this selection, what assumptions does the author make about the knowledge you have about his subject matter?

What background knowledge about the Depression do you bring to the reading?

DAY 5

If you were to interview Melvin Taylor, what five questions would you like to ask him?

Do you think teenagers can relate to individuals from Mr. Taylor's era?

_____

_____

_____

_____

_____

_____

Selection 20

Possible Student Responses

DAYS 1–5: *Writing response groups*

- Students will need specific instructions regarding the dynamics and structure of their writing-response groups. You may wish to have each group turn in one copy of the responses to the discussion questions, or you might require each student to write responses to the questions. These questions may be facilitated through a full-class discussion rather than through small-group responses.

Selection 21

1. Carroll chose a different route back to the camp, one that took them back through a burnt forest. (*The Piano Tuner,* Daniel Mason)

2. He had learned the worst lesson that life can teach—that it makes no sense. (*American Pastoral,* Philip Roth)

3. It was wretched weather; stormy and wet, stormy and wet; mud, mud, mud, deep in all the streets. (*Great Expectations,* Charles Dickens)

4. After five minutes, Lieutenant Jimmy Cross moved to the tunnel, leaned down, and examined the darkness. (*The Things They Carried,* Tim O'Brien)

5. He tried twice for the reverse gear, gave up and put it in forward, turning across the lawn and back on the driveway until he was facing the street. (*Sometimes a Great Notion,* Ken Kesey)

A good concluding paragraph ties the whole essay together.

Selection 21

Each day this week you will use a sentence from a well-known book as the first sentence of a paragraph you will create. Assume that each paragraph you write is the first paragraph of a separate short story or novel.

DAY 1

Write a paragraph that begins with sentence 1.

DAY 2

Write a paragraph that begins with sentence 2.

DAY 3

Write a paragraph that begins with sentence 3.

DAY 4

Write a paragraph that begins with sentence 4.

DAY 5

Write a paragraph that begins with sentence 5.

_____

_____

_____

_____

_____

_____

_____

_____

_____

_____

_____

_____

Selection 21

Possible Student Responses

DAYS 1–5: Generating effective ideas

- You might choose to have students share their paragraphs with last week's response. These paragraphs may be developed into short stories, if desired.

Selection 22

This week you will write cinquains. A cinquain (*cinq* is French for five) is a poem with a very specific form.

Line 1: two syllables
Line 2: four syllables
Line 3: six syllables
Line 4: eight syllables
Line 5: two syllables

Sample cinquain:

If you

Were to love me

Without knowing that I

Would never love you in return,

Would you?

When brainstorming ideas, think about the details that will help you to focus the topic.

Selection 22

Daily Student Prompts

DAY 1

As a class, create a cinquain about jealousy.

DAY 2

Select a topic of your choice and write a cinquain.

DAY 3

Rewrite the cinquain from Day 1 or 2 from the perspective of a child.

DAY 4

Write a cinquain about an aspect of school—without using the letter *a*.

DAY 5

Write a cinquain about a movie or television program. Try to capture the essence of the movie or program in your poem.

_____

_____

_____

_____

_____

_____

_____

_____

_____

_____

_____

_____

_____

Selection 22

Possible Student Responses

DAY 1: *Poetry—using writing models*

- You may wish to begin this week's activities by writing a cinquain to share with your students. Even though the cinquain's form seems simple, it is difficult to write one that has merit.

DAY 2: *Poetry—using writing models*

- You might wish to brainstorm topics if students have difficulty getting started.

DAY 3: *Poetry—using writing models/revision*

- Remind students that they should use the language of a child, and they must think like a child as they write this cinquain.

DAY 4: *Poetry—experimenting with form*

- Writing without using a specific letter is an exercise used by many creative writing teachers in writing seminars.

DAY 5: *Poetry—using writing models*

- Students may enjoy sharing today's cinquains with the class.

Selection 23

[1] If a wealthy person gave my school a large sum of money I would want the money to go to buying textbooks for every subject in every classroom. [2] One reason I think we need books for every subject in every classroom is so that students have a book to take home to refer to for homework. [3] Homework is not always very easy and when you really don't know how to do the homework, a book is nice to have to point you in the right direction and help you understand the work better also. [4] I also think having a book for every subject in the classroom would improve our statewide scores overall. [5] Books are essential for a good education because as you're reading to figure out how to do your work, you're also getting the reading skills you need. [6] If our school got a large sum of money I would want the money to go to buying textbooks for every subject in every classroom.

An essay has three basic components: an introduction, supporting paragraphs, and a conclusion.

Selection 23

Daily Student Prompts

This essay was written in response to the following prompt: "If someone were to give your school a large sum of money, how should the money be used?"

The six sentences comprise the entire essay. Your assignment this week is to rewrite the essay.

DAY 1

Expand sentence 1 into an introductory paragraph; you may change and improve this sentence as needed. (For your reference, sentences 2, 4, and 5 will act as the models for the topic sentences of the body paragraphs.)

DAY 2

Rewrite sentence 2 into a topic sentence for the first body paragraph of your essay. You may revise and edit as you deem necessary. Sentence 3 can also be used for this paragraph. Use specific examples in this paragraph to improve its clarity and specificity; perhaps you have personal experience you could use in this paragraph. Strengthen the verbs and attempt to use strong nouns rather than general nouns with accompanying adjectives.

DAY 3

Rewrite sentence 4 into a topic sentence for the second body paragraph of your essay. This paragraph certainly needs additional information and support!

DAY 4

Rewrite sentence 5 into a topic sentence for the third body paragraph of your essay. Again, this paragraph requires additional support and explanation.

DAY 5

The conclusion of the original essay was simply a restatement of the first sentence—not exactly a compelling conclusion. Write a conclusion for your essay. Generally, no new information will be introduced in this paragraph, but you should make a strong case for the assertion that the "donation" should go to the textbook budget. Reread and revise/edit your essay as needed.

Selection 23

<u>*Possible Student Responses*</u>

DAY 1: *Effective introduction/revision*

- The model essay is a typical underdeveloped essay written by many students for state writing assessments. Depending on the skill level of your students, you might wish to write a sample introductory paragraph for this week's assignment. Stronger writers should be able to develop a better paragraph on their own.

DAY 2: *Main idea/supporting details/revision*

- Encourage students to amend the content as well as the structure of the original essay. Most students should understand the structure of topic sentence, supporting evidence, and explanation. However, if students need to review this form, this might be a good opportunity to cover this format. Also, remind students that they can argue their points through logic, ethics, and compassion (*logos, ethos,* and *pathos*).

DAY 3: *Main idea/supporting details/revision*

- If your students are comfortable with peer editing, you might have students edit the first two revised paragraphs. Then they can proceed to write paragraph 3.

DAY 4: *Main idea/supporting details/revision*

- Even though the original essay falls into a five-paragraph format, students can certainly expand their essays into longer pieces, if desired.

DAY 5: *Effective conclusion/revision*

- Students are completely on their own when they write the conclusion. Stress that this is the writer's last opportunity to convince the reader to agree with him/her. When students have completed their essays, you may wish to copy some of the revisions and share them with the class.

Selection 24

1. Mr. Madison was unable to (elicit, illicit) any additional information about the dented fender from his son.

2. The G-Mass Communications Corporation announced that their merger with another communications giant was (eminent, imminent).

3. (Everyone, Every one) of the new students found the huge campus daunting, to say the least.

4. Mayla knew she had pushed her luck with her father (farther, further) than she should have.

5. There are (fewer, less) smokers in our state today than there were ten years ago.

6. "(First, Firstly), I would like to thank my coach for his support throughout this season."

7. The convicted murderer was (hanged, hung) the day after his last appeal was rejected.

8. The solution to the IT problem was (ingenious, ingenuous) and saved the company millions of dollars.

9. (In regards to, In regard to) your offer, I decline.

10. Bryce was (kind of, sort of) bored with the novel he had checked out of the library.

11. Cable television was the (media, medium) that received the best election coverage ratings.

12. Only a small (percent, percentage) of the legislators supported the bill to increase taxes.

13. "We will now (precede, proceed) to the next item on our agenda."

14. The overloaded bus skidded (toward, towards) the crowded intersection.

15. (Who, Whom) did the manager select to be his successor?

Selection 24

Daily Student Prompts

DAY 1

Select the correct word or phrase for sentences 1, 2, and 3.

DAY 2

Select the correct word or phrase for sentences 4, 5, and 6.

DAY 3

Select the correct word or phrase for sentences 7, 8, and 9.

DAY 4

Select the correct word or phrase for sentences 10, 11, and 12.

DAY 5

Select the correct word or phrase for sentences 13, 14, and 15.

Selection 24

<u>*Possible Student Responses*</u>

DAY 1: *Usage*

1. elicit

    Elicit means "to bring out," and *illicit* usually means "unlawful."

2. imminent

    Imminent means "about to happen," and *eminent* usually means "outstanding."

3. Every one

    Every one means "each individual," and *everyone* is an indefinite pronoun.

DAY 2: *Usage*

4. further

    Further usually means a "quantity or degree," and *farther* usually relates to a distance.

5. fewer

    Fewer usually relates to items that can be counted; *less* relates to general amounts.

6. First

    First (second, third, etc.) is preferred over *firstly, secondly, thirdly.*

DAY 3: *Usage*

7. hanged

    Hanged is the past and past-participle form of the verb "to hang" or "to execute." *Hung* is the past and past-participle of the verb *hang* which means "to suspend."

8. ingenious

    Ingenious usually means "clever," and *ingenuous* usually means "frank."

9. In regard to

    In regards to is an inaccurate representation of *in regard to* or *as regards.*

(continued)

Selection 24

DAY 4: *Usage*

10. Neither!

    Both *kind of* and *sort of* are incorrect when used to mean "somewhat."

11. medium

    Medium is the singular form of *media,* and the sample sentence refers to cable television (singular).

12. percentage

    Percentage is used with a description using *large* or *small; percent* (or *per cent)* is used with a specific number.

DAY 5: *Usage*

13. proceed

    Proceed usually means "to go forward," and *precede* usually means "to come before."

14. toward or towards

    Both terms are acceptable although sometimes *toward* is preferred.

15. Whom

    Whom is used as the object of the verb *select; who* is used for subjects and subject complements.

Selection 25

There is no writing selection for this week's assignment. This week you will create a description of a specific place. You can select a locale with which you are familiar, or you may create an imaginary place.

Daily Student Prompts

DAY 1

Select your locale and write a paragraph that describes its physical attributes.

DAY 2

Revise yesterday's paragraph or add information to yesterday's paragraph that creates a sense of time for your locale. You may use a season or a specific date or period of time. For example, you might write the description as if it were winter or set during the Civil War.

DAY 3

Introduce a person into your description. This individual might be a specific person or just an anonymous individual who appears in your locale.

DAY 4

Introduce a sound into your description. This sound may be a background noise or a prominent sound to which the reader's attention is drawn.

DAY 5

Introduce an event into your description that will attract the reader's attention (it may relate to the sound introduced on Day 4).

_____

_____

_____

_____

_____

_____

_____

_____

_____

Selection 25

Possible Student Responses

DAYS 1–5: *Generating effective ideas*

- The writing this week is meant to offer no-risk exercises that stimulate possible story starters or elements that might be expanded into short stories or poems. If you use writing-response groups (or pairs) in your class, students might enjoy receiving feedback from group members.

Selection 26

There is no writing sample for this week's exercises. Have fun with these exercises, and be ready to share your final product with the class.

Daily Student Prompts

DAY 1

Select a character from television, a movie, history, current politics, a cartoon (the character does not have to be human), or school that most of your classmates would know. If you choose an individual with very distinguishable characteristics or speech, this assignment will be more enjoyable. Describe this individual's physical characteristics in a well-written paragraph. **You may not use the character's name in your writing at any point this week.** You may write this assignment in either first person or third person. Try to be as detailed as possible.

DAY 2

Add a sense of place to your paragraph from Day 1. You don't necessarily need to place the character in a predictable place. In other words, if you were writing about a politician, you could place him in salsa class instead of his office. Be creative here.

DAY 3

Introduce dialogue in your paragraph (you might need to expand your writing to multiple paragraphs at this point). Think of your character's personality, and try to match his/her dialect to his/her personality. Of course, you could play with this aspect of the assignment and have your politician rap instead of just using straightforward dialog.

DAY 4

Edit and revise your writing. You might need to expand certain aspects of your work. For instance, you might develop your character's actions (maybe more about the politician's salsa class, for example). Remember, even though you might have used generous humor in your creation, hopefully your classmates will be able to recognize your character.

DAY 5

Share your writing products with a writing-response group or the entire class—whichever your instructor prefers.

Selection 26

Possible Student Responses

DAY 1: *Experimenting with language/paragraph development*

- This week's exercises should provide an enjoyable experience for students. Typically, they have no problem developing their character. Be prepared for some unpredictable writing products.

DAY 2: *Experimenting with language/setting*

- Today's assignment requires students to quickly create a recognizable locale for their characters. Even though these assignments may seem frivolous to students, it requires them to be specific and clear as they write.

DAY 3: *Experimenting with language/dialogue/characterization*

- Students may wish to introduce a second character with whom the main character can converse. Of course, the main character's speech could be in the form of internal thought, a monologue, or even a one-sided telephone call.

DAY 4: *Revision*

- Today students will refine their writing. You might wish to have students share their work with a classmate so they can have some feedback.

DAY 5: *Writing response group/sharing*

- Today students should share their compositions with the class and have students try to identify the original character. This could be a memorable experience, to say the least.

Selection 27

Each day this week, you will reflect on an aspect of your writing this school year. Your teacher may ask that you turn in your work as an assignment, or you may be requested to keep the work for your own reference.

Daily Student Prompts

DAY 1

Which *Daily Writing Fundamentals* exercise(s) did you find most beneficial? Why?

DAY 2

Which *Daily Writing Fundamentals* exercise(s) did you find least beneficial? How and why would you change the exercise(s)?

DAY 3

Which *Daily Writing Fundamentals* exercise(s) did you enjoy the most? What was enjoyable about the exercise(s)?

DAY 4

How has your writing improved this year? What type of writing or what elements of writing have matured the most? essays? creative writing? mechanics? revision? poetry? fluency? effective development?

DAY 5

What elements of your writing need the most improvement? What types of assignments can help your writing improve?

_____

_____

_____

_____

_____

_____

_____

_____

_____

Selection 27

Possible Student Responses

DAYS 1–5: *Reflection*

- This week's assignment might work best as one of the last exercises of the school year. Having students think about their writing is a critical element in writing maturation. If desired, you might wish to collect their work and use it for planning purposes. Or, you might instruct students to complete the week's assignments in their writing journals, if applicable.

Selection 28

[1] I think the most profound changes in a person happen not in one breathtaking instant, but in small, gradual changes that are realized late. [2] My most profound change came from overcoming my extreme passivity. [3] In middle school, I was always the quiet, shy girl who would always give in to her friends and various others just to make them happy. [4] I had the typical people pleaser personality. [5] Always willing to do for others and never willing to do for myself.

[6] Today, however, I tread the balance between passive and emphatic. [7] I made the transition to that glorious personality type that my ninth grade Life Management teacher so eloquently referred to as "assertive." [8] I am now a young woman who is content with herself and thus content with life.

[9] I used to allow my supposed best friends to make fun of me until it cut at my very core and still never made a peep one way or the other. [10] After a year of being cut down I put up a wall shielding me from hurtful words and people. [11] Despite my newly impenetrable force field, it didn't stop harmful words from exiting. [12] I took all of my pent up frustration and released it upon the undeserving. [13] I would cut others down to feel powerful just like my "friends" had done to me, but it had made me considerably more miserable than before.

[14] My life altering change did not occur in one brief moment of clarity or even in a week of ongoing meditation. [15] The crippling obstacle was defeated slowly throughout the course of three years. [16] My metamorphosis was proceeding at such snail paced speeds that I didn't even realize what was happening right before my eyes. [17] My partial self-actualization transpired when an old friend from middle school commented on how I was exceedingly "nicer than

(continued)

Selection 28

before" and "completely different from middle school." [18] That one comment took me off guard and caused me to ponder the meaning of his unexpected kind words.

[19] Change is the most essential thing in life, yet the hardest to fully accomplish. [20] I have made a drastic transition from my former suppressed and tired self to the vivacious and friendly person I am now. [21] I will take what I have learned from my transformation and use it as a guideline for future obstacles that may stand in my way.

—a student college application essay

The type of language used in a piece of writing can provide clues about the narrator.

Selection 28

Daily Student Prompts

DAY 1

Does the student write with a solid perception of his/her audience?

DAY 2

What are some examples of diction that show the maturity of the writer?

DAY 3

Are there any areas where the writer's argument is weakened?

DAY 4

How could the student have strengthened his/her argument?

DAY 5

Rewrite the ending of this essay in a way that makes a more persuasive argument.

_____

_____

_____

_____

_____

_____

_____

_____

_____

_____

_____

_____

_____

_____

_____

_____

Selection 28

<u>*Possible Student Responses*</u>

DAY 1: *Audience awareness*

- The student's diction and grammar show that he/she is aware of the audience for whom he/she writes. The writing is formal, with no slang, abbreviations, or informal conventions.

DAY 2: *Word choice*

- Among the words students may notice are: profound, passivity, emphatic, eloquently, shielding, impenetrable, crippling, metamorphosis, self-actualization, transpired, exceedingly, ponder, and vivacious.

DAY 3: *Supporting details*

- The statement that he/she "treads a balance between passive and emphatic" conveys the idea that the student has not really transformed him/herself. The writer provides no details of his/her change apart from one comment from a former friend.

DAY 4: *Supporting details*

- reword the "passive and emphatic" statement to better represent the change she has undergone
- provide more examples of how the change affected her life
- include more specifics in her conclusion as to how this change will help her in the future

DAY 5: *Effective conclusion/revision*

- Responses will vary, but should include specific ideas of how the change will impact his/her future.

Selection 29

July 10, 2006

Acme Products, Inc.
1234 Acme Place
Acme, FL 33552

To Whom It May Concern:

I am writing to tell you that your product, the Ultra CompuProtect stinks! What I want from you is a full refund and the replacement cost of my computer.

I used your bag (baggie is more like it) to carry my laptop on my vacation, and it didn't protect anything. In fact, my computer can now be used as a door stop, because it's not good for anything else. It looks as if someone took a sledgehammer to it. I took it to a computer repair shop and they laughed! It is now a worthless heap of junk, which is what you product is.

I'm sure that the fools who designed this thing are all sitting around laughing their heads off. Another sucker paid $299.95 for a bag that wouldn't protect a brick. What are you people thinking? You must hire idiots to design your products. Of course, that wouldn't happen if there weren't idiots doing the hiring!!!!

What I want from you is a refund for the piece-of-trash product I bought, and the replacement of my computer. And if I don't get it? You'll be hearing from my lawyer!

Sincerely,

Joe McAllister
1406 Winter St.
Hillview, NY 55103

Selection 29

Daily Student Prompts

DAY 1

Identify any problems with the form/layout of this business letter.

DAY 2

What is the problem with the salutation of the letter?

DAY 3

Does this writer understand to whom he is writing?

DAY 4

What did this writer do correctly?

DAY 5

Rewrite the letter so that it is likely to get a favorable response.

_____

_____

_____

_____

_____

_____

_____

_____

_____

_____

_____

_____

_____

_____

_____

_____

Selection 29

Possible Student Responses

DAY 1: *Business letter*

The writer has his layouts mixed. Two choices for a business letter are block and semi-block. He needs to conform to one of these.

BLOCK	SEMI-BLOCK	
Sender's address		Sender's address
Sender's address		Sender's address
Date		Date
Recipient's name	Recipient's name	
Recipient's address	Recipient's address	
Recipient's address	Recipient's address	
Salutation	Salutation	
Body of letter	Body of letter	
Closing		Closing
Sender's name		Sender's name

DAY 2: *Business letter*

- A business letter should be addressed to a particular person. With the availability of company information on the Internet, it is not difficult to find the name of the person to whom you are writing. If the name simply cannot be located, address the letter to the title. For example: Dear Chief Financial Officer.

DAY 3: *Audience awareness*

- No. If the writer's goal is to persuade the company to refund his money and replace his computer, he is going about it the wrong way. You do not insult those from whom you want something. His language should be more professional and less emotional.

DAY 4: *Business letter—organization*

- The contents required of this type of letter are present, just not written in the correct voice. The first paragraph contains the purpose of the letter, the body paragraphs contain details to support his purpose, and the last paragraph restates his purpose.

DAY 5: *Revision*

- Letters will vary. Students should be reminded to concentrate on the form and audience issues discussed this week.

Selection 30

¹ My long two-pointed ladder's sticking through a tree

² Toward heaven still,

³ And there's a barrel that I didn't fill

⁴ Beside it, and there may be two or three

⁵ Apples I didn't pick upon some bough.

⁶ But I am done with apple-picking now.

⁷ Essence of winter sleep is on the night,

⁸ The scent of apples: I am drowsing off.

⁹ I cannot rub the strangeness from my sight

¹⁰ I got from looking through a pane of glass

¹¹ I skimmed this morning from the drinking trough

¹² And held against the world of hoary grass.

¹³ It melted, and I let it fall and break.

¹⁴ But I was well

¹⁵ Upon my way to sleep before it fell,

¹⁶ And I could tell

¹⁷ What form my dreaming was about to take.

¹⁸ Magnified apples appear and disappear,

¹⁹ Stem end and blossom end,

²⁰ And every fleck of russet showing clear.

²¹ My instep arch not only keeps the ache,

²² It keeps the pressure of a ladder-round.

²³ I feel the ladder sway as the boughs bend.

²⁴ And I keep hearing from the cellar bin

(continued)

Selection 30

[25] The rumbling sound

[26] Of load on load of apples coming in.

[27] or I have had too much

[28] Of apple-picking: I am overtired

[29] Of the great harvest I myself desired.

[30] There were ten thousand thousand fruit to touch,

[31] Cherish in hand, lift down, and not let fall.

[32] For all

[33] That struck the earth,

[34] No matter if not bruised or spiked with stubble,

[35] Went surely to the cider-apple heap

[36] As of no worth.

[37] One can see what will trouble

[38] This sleep of mine, whatever sleep it is.

[39] Were he not gone,

[40] The woodchuck could say whether it's like his

[41] Long sleep, as I describe its coming on

[42] Or just some human sleep.

—*After Apple-picking* by Robert Frost

Selection 30

Daily Student Prompts

DAY 1

What images does Frost use to make the act of apple picking vivid?

DAY 2

What type of images does Frost use? Place the images into categories.

DAY 3

The speaker uses the word sleep six times. How does this repetition affect the meaning of the poem? How does the speaker feel about this sleep?

DAY 4

How would the meaning have been affected if the speaker had used past tense instead of present?

DAY 5

Rewrite this poem as a piece of prose.

_____

_____

_____

_____

_____

_____

_____

_____

_____

_____

_____

_____

_____

Selection 30

Possible Student Responses

DAY 1: *Figurative language—imagery*

- Some of the images students may point out include the following:

  "two-pointed ladder's sticking through a tree"

  "a barrel that I didn't fill"

  "two or three / Apples I didn't pick upon some bough"

  "world of hoary grass"

  "stem and blossom end"

  "every fleck of russet"

  "My instep arch not only keeps the ache / It keeps the pressure of a ladder-round"

  "I feel the ladder sway"

  "The rumbling sound / Of load on load of apples coming in"

  "ten thousand thousand fruit to touch"

  "bruised or spiked with stubble"

  "cider-apple heap"

  "The scent of apples"

DAY 2: *Figurative language—imagery*

- The images are visual, auditory, touch, and olfactory, and some serve as a combination. Responses may vary, depending on perception.
- Visual: 1, 3, 10, 13, 18, 20, 30, 34
- Auditory: 24, 25
- Touch: 21, 23, 31
- Olfactory: 8

DAY 3: *Repetition*

- Students should recognize that the repetition of a word is significant. In this poem, they may notice that the speaker is satisfied with his labor, but tired. He has picked thousands upon thousands of apples—his life's work—and is ready to rest. Along with the fact that this is winter, a time for nature to rest, they may see that he is thinking of his death, not just a good night's rest.

(continued)

Selection 30

Possible Student Responses

DAY 4: *Analyzing writing/verb tense*

- If sleep is indeed meant as death, the poem written in the past tense would have a totally different feel. Here, we are in the moment; there is an immediacy of a man facing his mortality, while contemplating his life's work. He is in the present, but looking toward what awaits him in the future. If the speaker had been looking back, where would he be? Already dead? It would have been a different poem, perhaps remarking on immortality and what lies beyond instead of what is.

DAY 5: *Prose*

- Responses will vary. Remind students to try and use repetition to make a point.

Selection 31

¹ In Daniel Anderson's, "Sunflowers in a Field," Anderson uses imagery and diction to create a tone of uplifting assurance. ² This tone changes from upbeat and hopeful to indifferent. ³ This shift in tone accurately displays the apathy mankind naturally possesses.

⁴ First, Anderson uses imagery to create an uplifting tone of assurance. ⁵ The descriptions of the sunflowers and goldfinches are upbeat and attractive. ⁶ The goldfinches are described as being like "drizzled lemon drops (and) like lozenges of candied yellow light." ⁷ Through this, an image of the gold finch is portrayed as bright and gentle. ⁸ In slight contrast, the sunflowers are described as "fires, like silk coronas blazing west." ⁹ It can be concluded that the sunflowers are a little more forceful than the "soft" goldfinches. ¹⁰ Through these contrasting images in nature, humans are assured that they can live their lives "with greater sympathy." ¹¹ The images of the birds with the sunflowers create a pleasant relation with humans and nature. ¹² Through this relation, people can gain more insight into themselves, as well as the world around them. ¹³ This in turn, gives them "greater sympathy" for nature as well as man kind.

¹⁴ Furthermore, Anderson's use of imagery produces a tone of indifference. ¹⁵ For example, image of the "pewter cold-front clouds" signals the end of the "resolution" to live life with "greater sympathy" as well as the end of the goldfinches and sunflowers. ¹⁶ This image suggests that when an event occurs that would appear to inhibit man from attaining a "resolution" that the average man or woman would take an apathetic approach and abandon their promise.

¹⁷ Not only does the imagery reinforce the tone of indifference, but the diction does as well. ¹⁸ The speaker notes that people are

(continued)

Selection 31

"intent on picking up the telephone" to speak with friends. [19] The word "intent" suggests that one may desire to fulfill a promise, however, there is no guarantee that one will succeed. [20] Furthermore, the speaker notes one will "vow to never, ever, ever" allow distance to grow between them and their friend. [21] The repetition of "ever" portrays the passion one's resolution possesses. [22] However, "sleep settles just a little more." [23] Through this it is suggested that with a "little" drowsiness one succumbs to apathy. [24] Therefore, people seem to settle with calling "perhaps some other time." [25] The word "perhaps" is uncertain. [26] This, also, strengthens the idea that the task will never be accomplished.

[27] Through Anderson's use of imagery, it can be concluded that the first tone portrayed is hopeful and upbeat. [28] The peaceful coexistence of two. [29] Somewhat contrasting things give humans assurance that they will have the ability to accomplish personal resolutions. [30] Anderson's diction and imagery also shifts the tone. [31] To one of indifference. [32] The images of vanishing goldfinches takes away the assurance instilled in humans. [33] Thus, leaving them with indifference and apathy.

Writers must edit their essays. When checking over your work, don't forget to look for and fix errors in capitalization, punctuation, grammar, and spelling.

Selection 31

Daily Student Prompts

DAY 1

Is the introduction of the essay effective? Why or why not?

DAY 2

On the whole, is the organization of the essay effective?

DAY 3

Are there areas in the essay which do not fully support the claims of the writer?

DAY 4

Identify the sentence fragments in the conclusion. Did the writer use these intentionally for effect, or are they errors?

DAY 5

Rewrite the conclusion, correcting the sentence fragments.

Selection 31

Possible Student Responses

DAY 1: *Effective introduction*

- The introduction is confusing in that it states that the tone is one of "uplifting assurance," then talks about a shift in tone. It is more effective to present the tone as changing from the beginning. Also, the term "uplifting assurance" is unusual and difficult to define.

DAY 2: *Organization*

- There are problems with the introduction and conclusion, but they co-exist. The writer uses transitions effectively, and provides support for his/her assertions. Overall, the organization is effective.

DAY 3: *Supporting details*

- Responses will vary, but the following are two examples students may notice:

  The statement "humans are assured that they can live their lives 'with greater sympathy' " is not fully supported by the details on the flowers and birds.

  "[T]he speaker notes one will 'vow to never, ever, ever' allow distance to grow between them and their friend" does not support the idea of indifference, and could be left out.

DAY 4: *Sentence structure—fragments*

- "The peaceful coexistence of two."
- "To one of indifference."
- "Thus, leaving them with indifference and apathy."
- The author used sentence fragments unintentionally, and should revise these sentences to eliminate the fragment.

DAY 5: *Revision/sentence fragments*

- Responses will vary, but the above fragments should be corrected.

Selection 32

¹ Last night I watched a starving child cry.

² I could see the sharp outline of his bones jutting out from beneath his taught skin—his rib cage heaving visibly as the sobs shook his poor, fragile body. ³ I saw his swollen belly and the way his limbs hung limply at his sides, like broken twigs. ⁴ But what stayed with me were his eyes. ⁵ Sunken and shadowed in their sockets, his tears seeming to glitter from the depths of some profound emotion that I could not seem to grasp or understand. ⁶ I watched as they carved shiny, silver traces through the dust on his cheeks, and for a brief moment I wondered whether he could really see me.

⁷ Seconds later he was gone—replaced by the image of a dancing Coca-Cola can as the news broadcast switched over to a commercial.

⁸ And I sat there, mulling over his predicament while wondering whether or not to start my Calculus homework. ⁹ To me, he was nothing more than a poster child, and I had homework to do.

¹⁰ You ask me what confuses me in life. I'll tell you. ¹¹ I'm confused by the fact that I sleep in a two-story, four-bedroom house while an African family of twelve huddles in a dilapidated old shack made of sticks and mud. ¹² I'm confused by the fact that I'm five pounds overweight whereas others haven't seen a bite of food in over a week. ¹³ I'm confused by the fact that the bracelet I wear around my wrist could support a child for over a month. I'm confused by the fact that I watched that helpless little boy cry—and didn't shed a tear.

¹⁴ I wonder when I changed, when I became so devoid of human emotion that I could look misery in the eye and merely

(continued)

Selection 32

shrug my shoulders. ¹⁵ Tough break, kid! ¹⁶ Life's rough. ¹⁷ When I think about it, I frighten myself. ¹⁸ It seems as though there's a side of me that I didn't even know existed—one that has become so numb to the tragedies of this world that it no longer feels the tug of simple human kindness. ¹⁹ I can rant and rave about the injustices of this world until I'm blue in the face . . . I can spout out Bible verses about love and charity until my voice turns hoarse . . . But the fact remains the same: I didn't cry. ²⁰ That confuses me.

²¹ That night as I lay in bed, the boy's image flashed before me again in my mind. ²² And suddenly it occurred to me: he has a name. ²³ In that single, swift instant, something inside of me seemed to give way. ²⁴ He was a real person, flesh and blood— living under the same sky, sleeping under the same moon. ²⁵ It's hard to force yourself to see something you are so willing to ignore. ²⁶ It's easier to spare yourself the pain than embrace the truth. ²⁷ But at that moment I knew that I was helpless to change the reality before me. ²⁸ That boy had gone to bed hungry.

Imagery and descriptive words paint a picture for the reader.

Selection 32

Daily Student Prompts

DAY 1

Is the voice of this writer clear? What elements of the essay bring this out?

DAY 2

Is this piece fluent? There are two places where the writer uses particularly short sentences. What effect does this produce?

DAY 3

The writer uses a couple of clichés. Does this weaken her statement?

DAY 4

This piece does not follow the general form of a persuasive essay. Is it still persuasive? What makes it so?

DAY 5

Write a response to this writer. What about her essay made you consider your own reactions to the treatment of world problems/disasters in the media?

_____

_____

_____

_____

_____

_____

_____

_____

_____

_____

_____

_____

_____

_____

Selection 32

<u>*Possible Student Responses*</u>

DAY 1: *Voice*

- Yes, this piece has a strong voice. Elements that bring the author's voice out are the first person viewpoint, her apparent sincerity in examining her reactions to the broadcast, and the view we are given of her inner thought process. The specific details she gives about the child also help to pull the reader into the essay.

DAY 2: *Sentence structure*

- The essay is very fluent with a variety of sentence structures and syntax. The second paragraph from the end contains two pairs of short sentences: "Tough break, kid! Life's rough." and "I didn't cry. That confuses me." These sentences, so different from the others, stand out for effect. They make the reader slow down and feel her anger and confusion. They mimic the emotions and thoughts she is expressing.

DAY 3: *Word choice*

- In the second to last paragraph, the writer uses the phrases: "tug of simple human kindness" and "until I'm blue in the face." These could probably be expressed differently to greater effect, but because of the strength of the rest of the essay, they do not detract much from her message.

DAY 4: *Persuasion/form*

- This piece is a good example of an essay that does not follow a strict format, but nevertheless, fulfills its purpose. While the writer does not make an explicit call for action, her strong voice, and the details both of the news report and her own thoughts, bring across her message quite emphatically.

DAY 5: *Writing response*

- Responses will vary. Instruct students to cite details from the story that made an impact, and to provide details that support their reactions.

Share Your Bright Ideas

We want to hear from you!

Your name_____Date_____

School name_____

School address_____

City _____State _____Zip_____Phone number (_____)_____

Grade level(s) taught_____Subject area(s) taught_____

Where did you purchase this publication?_____

In what month do you purchase a majority of your supplements?_____

What moneys were used to purchase this product?

___School supplemental budget   ___Federal/state funding   ___Personal

Please "grade" this Walch publication in the following areas:

	A	B	C	D
Quality of service you received when purchasing	A	B	C	D
Ease of use	A	B	C	D
Quality of content	A	B	C	D
Page layout	A	B	C	D
Organization of material	A	B	C	D
Suitability for grade level	A	B	C	D
Instructional value	A	B	C	D

COMMENTS:_____

_____

What specific supplemental materials would help you meet your current—or future—instructional needs?

_____

Have you used other Walch publications? If so, which ones?_____

May we use your comments in upcoming communications?   ___Yes   ___No

Please **FAX** this completed form to **888-991-5755**, or mail it to

Customer Service, Walch Publishing, P. O. Box 658, Portland, ME 04104-0658

We will send you a **FREE GIFT** in appreciation of your feedback. **THANK YOU!**